D1540577

INTRODUCTION

Senses at work

Every day we look at scenes and screens and listen to sounds such as music and people speaking. We smell scents and odors, eat tasty meals, and embrace a loved one or stroke a pet. Yet we rarely pause to wonder how we are able to do all these activities, or how the body's senses work to receive information about the world around us.

A stimulating event: the body's senses respond to the loud music, bright lights, sweaty smells, and moving crowds at this nightclub.

CONTENTS

THE SENSES

Steve Parker

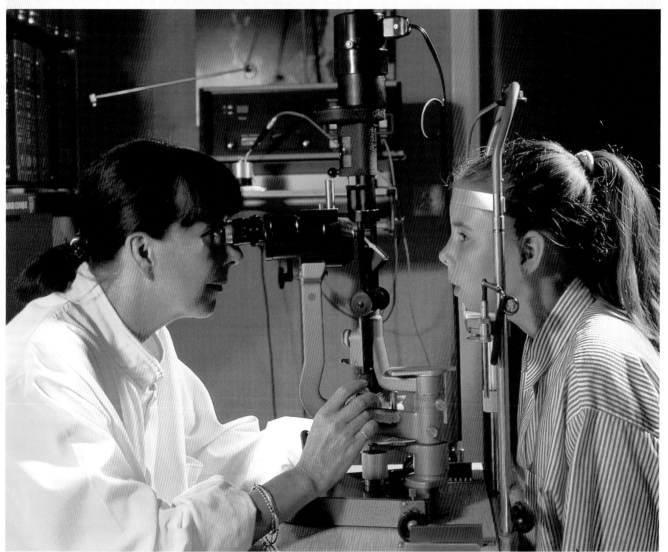

Raintree

Chicago, Illinois

Titles in the series:

The Brain and Nervous System • Di
The Heart, Lungs, and Blood • Reproduction
The Senses • The Skeleton and Muscles

© 2004 Raintree
Published by Raintree, a divison of Reed Elsevier, Inc.
Chicago, Illinois
Customer Service 888-363-4266
Visit our website at www.raintreelibrary.com

For information address the publisher:
Raintree, 100 N. LaSalle, Suite 1200, Chicago, IL 60602

Library of Congress Cataloging-in-Publication Data:

Parker, Steve.
  The senses / Steve Parker.
      v. cm. -- (Our bodies)
Includes bibliographical references and index.
Contents: Eyes and sight -- The mind's eye -- Hear, ear -- What's that noise -- Sense scents.
  ISBN 0-7398-6624-9 (lib. bdg. : hc)
  1. Senses and sensation--Juvenile literature. [1. Senses and sensation.] I. Title. II. Series.
  QP434.P378 2004
  612.8--dc21
                          2003010549

08 07 06 05 04
10 9 8 7 6 5 4 3 2 1

Picture Acknowledgments
Front Cover (main image) Corbis (Charles Gupton); front cover (inset), p.9 Science Photo Library (Omikron; pp. 1, 16 Science Photo Library (CC Studio); p. 4 Corbis (Bojan Brecelji); p. 5 Alamy (ImageState); p. 7 Corbis (Stephen Frink)p. 9 (top) Digital Vision; p. 10 Science Photo Library (Andrew McClenaghan); pp. 13 (top), 21 (bottom), 25 Science Photo Library (Jamkes King-Holmes); p.13 bottom Science Photo Library (Ralph Eagle); p. 15 (top) FLPA (Tony Hamblin); p. 17 Science Photo Library (Stanford Eye Clinic); p. 18 Alamay (Jim Pickerell/Stock Connection, Inc.); p. 19 (bottom) Robert Harding Picture Library (Adam Woolfitt); p.22 Alamy (Wilmar Photography.com); p.23 (top) Corbis Digital Stock (Marty Snyderman); p. 24 Rex Features (Reso); pp. 26, 29 Science Photo Library (BSIP Vem); p. 31 Minden Pictures; p. 37 Science Photo Library (J C Revy); p. 38 Action Plus (Neil Tingle); p. 39 Science Photo Library (Astrid and Hanns-Frieder Michler); p. 41 Alamy (Novastock/Stock Connection Inc); p. 42 Rex Features (Clive Dixon); p. 44 Corbis (Bob Krist); p. 45 Robert Harding Picture Library (Vaughan Bean).

If one sense is faulty or lacking, another may be able to compensate—as in Braille, the touch-reading system for those with poor or no vision.

Five main senses

The body's five main senses are sight, hearing, smell, taste, and touch. Each of these major senses has body parts called sense organs, or sensors. They are specialized to detect a feature or change outside the body. For example, in sight, the eyes detect light rays, and in hearing, the ears pick up sound waves. The nose is sensitive to tiny odor particles, called **odorants,** floating in air, while the tongue detects flavor particles in food.

Signals to the brain

As the sense organs detect these features outside the body, they produce patterns of tiny electrical pulses, called **nerve** signals, inside the body. These signals are sent along nerves to the brain, which sorts and processes them. It is not in the sense organ itself but rather in the brain that we become aware of what our senses detect and realize what is happening around us.

More senses

The body's senses are much more complicated than they seem. For example, the skin is the sense organ of touch, or feeling, but it detects far more than physical contact with objects when it is touched or pressed. It can also feel heat, cold, movements, and pain. Balance is sometimes also called a sense, but it is really a process that goes on all the time, using information from various sense organs such as the skin, eyes, inner ears, and also tiny stretch sensors in muscles and joints.

EYES AND SIGHT

Most important

For most people, sight, or vision, is the most important sense. Closing your eyes makes it hard to move around safely or carry out everyday tasks such as writing, and it is impossible to read or watch television. More than half the knowledge and information in the brain, stored as memories, probably came in through the eyes as pictures, scenes, and other sights.

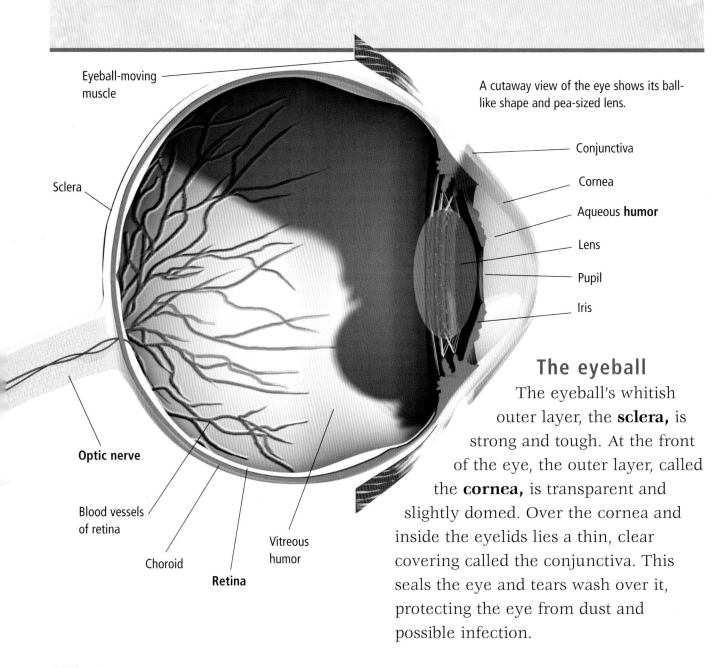

Eyeball-moving muscle

A cutaway view of the eye shows its ball-like shape and pea-sized lens.

Sclera

Conjunctiva

Cornea

Aqueous **humor**

Lens

Pupil

Iris

Optic nerve

Blood vessels of retina

Choroid

Vitreous humor

Retina

The eyeball

The eyeball's whitish outer layer, the **sclera,** is strong and tough. At the front of the eye, the outer layer, called the **cornea,** is transparent and slightly domed. Over the cornea and inside the eyelids lies a thin, clear covering called the conjunctiva. This seals the eye and tears wash over it, protecting the eye from dust and possible infection.

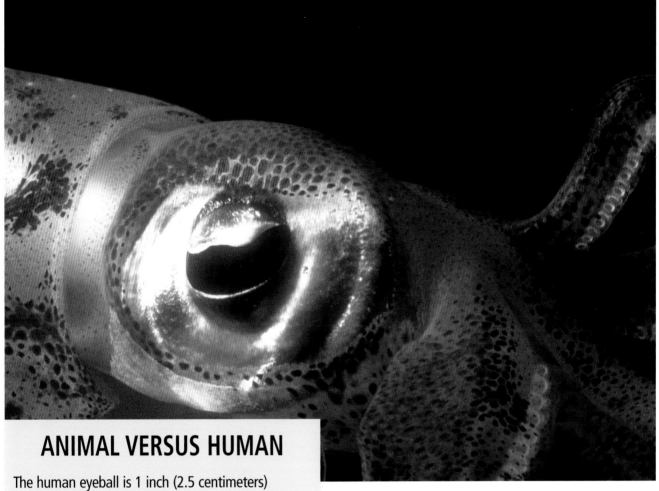

ANIMAL VERSUS HUMAN

The human eyeball is 1 inch (2.5 centimeters) across. The giant squid has the largest animal eye: It can be almost 8 inches (20 centimeters) across. Squid have huge eyes so that they can see well in the dark depths of the ocean.

Pupil and lens

Located behind the cornea, the **iris** is a colored ring composed mainly of muscle. The dark-looking hole in the middle is the **pupil.** The iris adjusts the size of the pupil according to light conditions. Usually the pupil gets larger in dim light to allow more light into the eye and give a brighter view. Just behind the pupil is the lens. Like the lens in a camera, it focuses the light rays to form a clear, sharp picture inside the eyeball (see next page).

Try this!

Study your own eyes in a mirror, looking for the sclera (white), iris (colored part), and pupil (dark hole). Close your eyes for fifteen seconds, then open them and carefully watch the pupil. With the eye closed, the pupil opens wider, trying to let in more light. As soon as the eye opens, the iris makes the pupil shrink, preventing too much light from entering.

DETECTING LIGHT

Light rays to nerve signals

Light rays shine into the eye through the clear **cornea** at the front and then through the hole called the **pupil** and the clear, curved lens behind it. Between the cornea and lens is a narrow space filled with fluid called aqueous **humor,** which is continually being made and absorbed. Then, the light passes into the middle of the eyeball. This is filled with a clear, jelly-like fluid called vitreous humor, which gives the eyeball its rounded shape and slightly squishy feel.

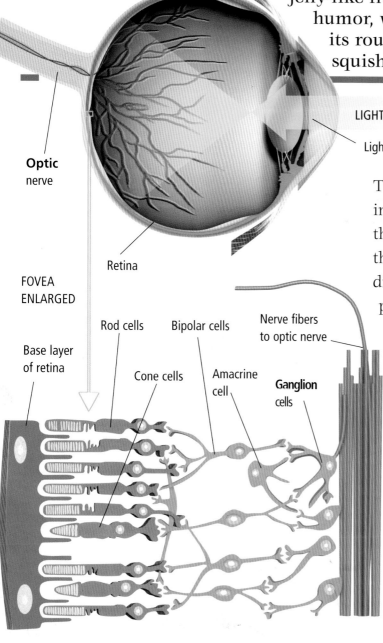

Optic nerve

Retina

FOVEA ENLARGED

Base layer of retina

Rod cells

Cone cells

Bipolar cells

Amacrine cell

Nerve fibers to optic nerve

Ganglion cells

LIGHT RAYS

Light rays pass through pupil and lens

The rays then shine onto the curved inner lining of the eyeball, known as the **retina.** This is the part that changes the energy from light rays, with their different colors and brightness, into patterns of **nerve** signals that are sent to the brain. Between the retina and the eye's tough outer covering (the **sclera**) is a middle layer called the choroid. This layer has many blood vessels that help to nourish the retina and sclera.

LIGHT RAYS

A series of cell layers in the retina process nerve signals from the rods and cones.

Inside the retina

The retina is bowl-shaped, about twice the area of a fingernail, and as thick as this piece of paper. Yet it contains many millions of microscopic parts called **rod cells** and **cone** cells. These make nerve signals when light rays shine onto them. The 125 million rod cells are spread evenly through most of the retina. Most of the seven million cone cells are packed closely into a tiny area known as the **fovea,** or yellow spot, in the middle of the retina at the back of the eye. When the eye looks directly at an object, the image of the object shines onto the fovea. This is the area of the retina where vision is clearest and sharpest, because the numerous closely packed cones can detect colors and tiny details (see next page).

MICRO BODY

In the retina the cone cells are slightly shorter and have pointed ends, while the rod cells are longer with blunter ends. Most of the cones are packed into a tiny area called the fovea, which is in the middle of the retina, facing the lens and pupil.

Cone cells (greenish) nestle among the taller rod cells (blue).

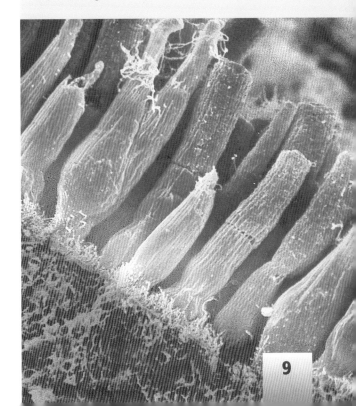

MOVEMENTS AND COLORS

Fast-changing images

The word "movies" comes from "moving pictures." However, the pictures are not really moving. In fact, they are still images, like photographs, that are flashed onto the screen very quickly, one after the other—25 or 30 of them every second. Each picture, or frame, is slightly different from the one before. But the light-sensitive **rod** and **cone cells** in the eye's **retina** cannot work fast enough to detect the pictures as single still images. As a result, the fast-changing images merge or blend together and give the impression of continuous movement.

Three colors for cones

The rod cells in the retina do not distinguish any colors, but instead detect all colors equally. They do distinguish different light levels, from bright to dull, and so they see in black and white. The cone cells are specialized to detect colors. There are three types of cone cells: red, green, and blue. These are not the colors of the cones themselves, but the colors of light they detect. For example, pure red light makes only the "red" cones work;

Problems with color vision can be detected using special charts made of dots with different hues. The most common form of color blindness is being unable to distinguish between certain shades of red and green in dim light (see page 17).

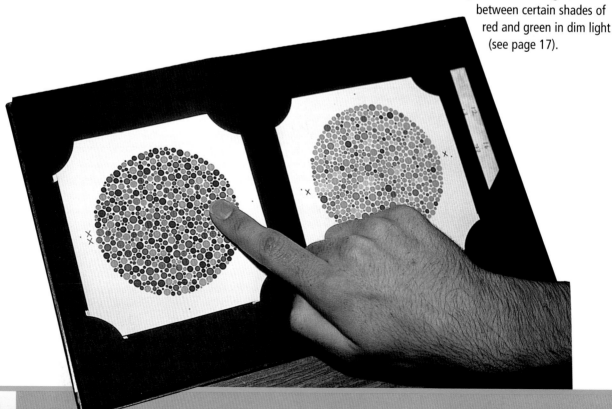

pure green light affects only "green" cones; and pure blue light causes "blue" cones to make **nerve** signals. Other colors of light are made up of mixtures of red, green, and blue light, and so they make combinations of cone cells work. For example, yellow light is a mixture of red and green light, so it makes red and green cones work at the same time. The brain figures out the colors and shades of light from the varying combinations of signals sent to it by the different types of cones.

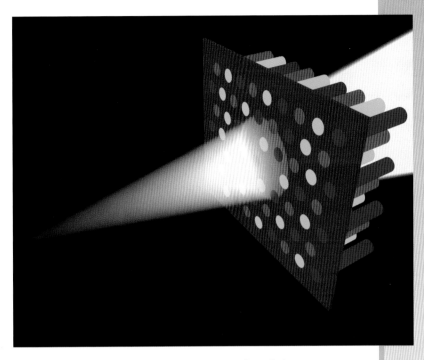

White light is a mixture of all colors, so it makes all three kinds of cone cells in the retina respond: red, green, and blue.

Make a flicker-drawing that is simple and easy to copy from one page to the next.

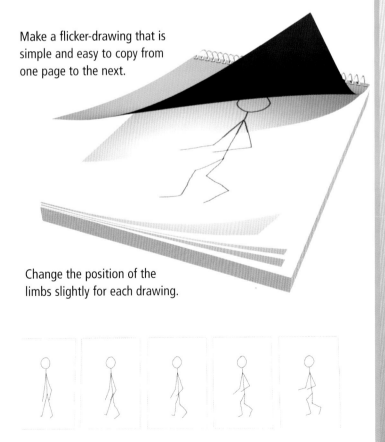

Change the position of the limbs slightly for each drawing.

Try this!

In a small notebook or notepad, draw a simple image such as a stick-person in the middle or lower corner of each page. Move the arms and legs slightly from one page to the next, as if the person is walking. When you flick the pages slowly, the eye can detect each picture separately. When you flick them faster, see how the stick-person seems to move more smoothly as the eye merges the images together. This is what happens when we watch television and movies.

DISTANCE AND DEPTH

Judging distance

We use our eyes to see colors, shapes, patterns, and movements, and also to judge distances. When we look at an object, both eyes point straight toward it. If the object is very close, the eyes must point slightly inward. The nearer the object, the greater the inward angle of each eye, which is called the angle of **convergence** (see image below).

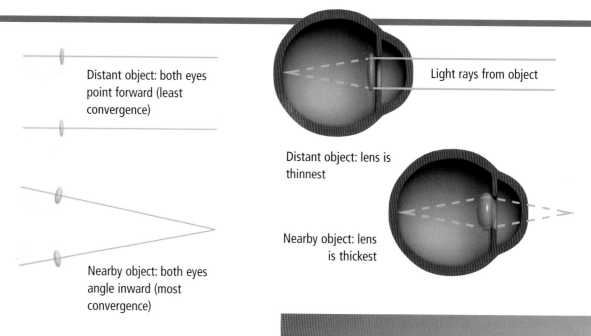

Distant object: both eyes point forward (least convergence)

Nearby object: both eyes angle inward (most convergence)

Light rays from object

Distant object: lens is thinnest

Nearby object: lens is thickest

The angle at which the eyes point inward is known as convergence, while the lens' changing shape for focusing is called accommodation. Both help us to assess distance.

The eyeball is moved by six tiny muscles behind it. These muscles have sensors in them to detect how short or long they get. As the eyes swivel to look inward at a nearby object, the muscles on the outside of the eye are stretched longer, and the brain detects this. It can then figure out the eye's angle of convergence to help judge the distance of the object.

Try this!

See how the eyes swivel and change their angle of convergence to judge distance. Have a friend hold a pen at arm's length and look straight at it, and then gradually move the pen closer. See how the friend's eyes gradually look inward more and more. When the pen is very close, the angle of convergence is greatest—and your friend looks "cross-eyed"!

Two eyes

The two eyes look at an object from different positions, so they have slightly different views of it. You can see this if you look at a nearby object with one eye only, then with the other eye. Notice how the two views are slightly different. The nearer the object, the more different the two views of it. The brain compares the two images and this also helps to judge its distance.

Frequent eye tests are part of the many checkups undergone by pilots, who must be able to see clearly both distant objects, such as the runway, and nearer ones, such as the dials and controls.

MICRO BODY

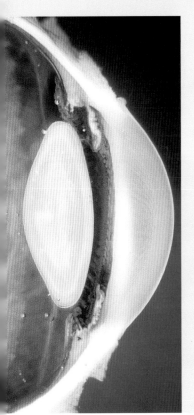

A camera's lens moves its position to focus the image clearly. The eye's lens does not move, but it does become fatter or thinner. The lens is suspended by tiny thread-like ligaments within a ring of muscle, the ciliary muscle, that alters its shape.

Tiny, shadowy, pale threads of ciliary ligaments link the yellow-colored lens to the pale brown bulges of ciliary muscle.

Looking through the lens

A camera's lens is adjusted to give a clear, sharp view of a nearby object or a faraway one. This is called focusing. The eye also adjusts its lens to focus on near or far objects. This is known as accommodation. The eye's lens focuses by changing its shape. A ring-shaped ciliary muscle around the lens contracts to make the ring smaller and the lens more bulging, so that it can focus on nearby objects. To focus on faraway objects, the ciliary muscle relaxes into a larger ring and stretches the lens thinner. Like the eye-moving muscles, the ciliary muscles have stretch sensors in them. Signals from these sensors pass to the brain, which can determine the shape of the lens and thus help judge the distance of the object.

THE MIND'S EYE

A complicated network

The eye's millions of **rods** and **cones** produce billions of **nerve** signals every second. These do not go straight to the brain, however. The rods and cones are connected to a layer of nerve **cells** in the **retina** known as bipolar cells, which are, in turn, linked to another layer, the **ganglion** cells. Still more cells link groups of rods and cones, as well as groups of ganglion cells. All these cells are within the retina. The result is an amazingly complicated network that works like a computer to process and combine nerve signals (see also page 8).

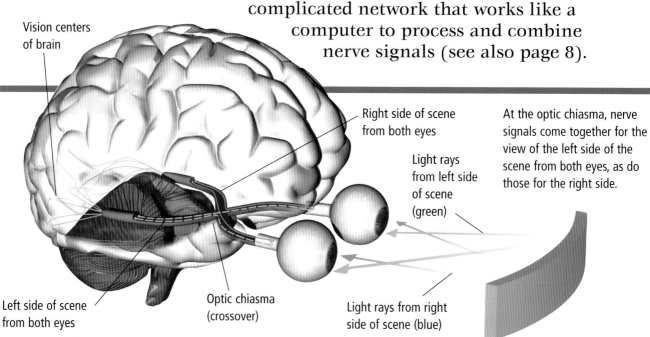

Vision centers of brain

Right side of scene from both eyes

Light rays from left side of scene (green)

At the optic chiasma, nerve signals come together for the view of the left side of the scene from both eyes, as do those for the right side.

Left side of scene from both eyes

Optic chiasma (crossover)

Light rays from right side of scene (blue)

From eye to brain

The nerve signals from all over the retina travel along about a million nerve fibers. These come together in one small area to form the start of the **optic** nerve. This area of the retina has no rods or cones, so it cannot detect light. It is known as the "blind spot." In daily life, the eyes dart about rapidly, and so the missing patch of the scene (the blind spot) is continually "filled in" and we do not notice it.

Try this!

Hold this page about a foot away from you. With one eye closed, look straight at the "x" (below) with the other eye. Gradually bring it closer. Keep looking at the "x," but also notice the dot (below, left), which disappears when it falls in your eye's blind spot.

● **X**

Inside the brain

The optic nerves join to the lower front of the brain, at what is called the optic chiasma. Here, nerve signals from one eye are "shared" with signals from the other eye. This makes it easier for the brain to compare the views in both eyes. The signals then pass to the lower rear brain surface, known as the visual **cortex,** or vision centers. This area decodes the signals from shapes, colors, lines, angles, curves, and shades, and puts them together as the final scene.

ANIMAL VERSUS HUMAN

Animal eyes work in various ways. The frog's eye has rod cells grouped into patches called "bug detectors." These are specialized to detect small, fast-moving objects such as flies. They cannot detect objects that do not move quickly, and so a stationary fly is safe until it moves.

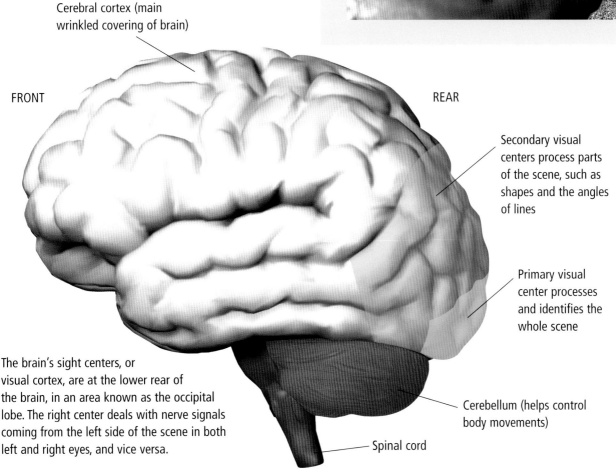

Cerebral cortex (main wrinkled covering of brain)

FRONT

REAR

Secondary visual centers process parts of the scene, such as shapes and the angles of lines

Primary visual center processes and identifies the whole scene

The brain's sight centers, or visual cortex, are at the lower rear of the brain, in an area known as the occipital lobe. The right center deals with nerve signals coming from the left side of the scene in both left and right eyes, and vice versa.

Cerebellum (helps control body movements)

Spinal cord

VISION PROBLEMS

A precious sense

Eyes are very delicate, and sight is very important. For a person who could previously see well, loss of sight can have enormous and restricting effects on everyday life. It is important to have a regular eye examination. This is usually done by a doctor called an **optometrist,** who can shine a light through the **pupil** to see the **retina** within.

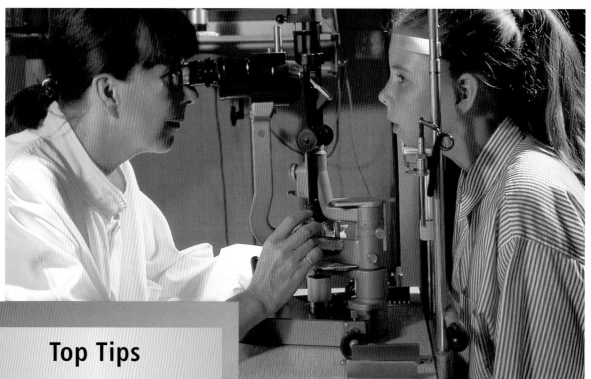

The optometrist uses various machines to check the eye's health, including the pressure inside the eyeball.

Top Tips

The eyes are at risk from fast-moving objects such as a ball in sports, windblown sand or grit, or tiny sharp pieces or shards when using equipment such as a metal-grinding machine. The risk of injury can be greatly reduced by wearing eye protection such as a mask.

Sight disorders

Some vision problems occur because the lens is the wrong shape in relation to the whole eyeball. In nearsightedness (myopia), the eyeball is too large for the lens, so the person cannot see faraway objects clearly. In farsightedness (hypermetropia), the eyeball is too small in relation to the lens, so nearby objects look blurred. An extra contact or eyeglass lens helps the eye's own lens to focus more clearly. About 8 in 100 males and 1 in 200 females are "color blind." Usually this means they cannot distinguish between two colors, most often red and green, because of an inherited fault with their **cone cells.** It is very rare to see no colors at all but only shades of gray.

Glaucoma, cataract, and diabetes

In glaucoma, too much fluid (aqueous **humor**) collects beneath the cornea. This increases the pressure in the eyeball and can damage the retina. In a cataract, the lens becomes opaque and looks white or "misty." Both disorders are more common in older people and can usually be treated successfully, especially with high-precision laser surgery. Diabetes is a condition in which the body is unable to use its main energy source, blood sugar, properly. It can damage small blood vessels in various parts of the body,

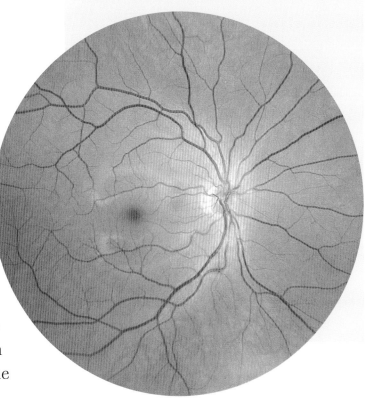

including the retina. Regular eye exams and careful control of diabetes can lessen the risk of this eye problem, known as diabetic retinopathy.

EARS AND HEARING

An automatic filter

Sound travels as waves through the air, water, and objects. It is detected by the organs of hearing or auditory sense: our ears. We do not notice or remember every sound we hear, however. The brain automatically filters out common and familiar sounds that are less important, such as the background noise of traffic or the wind. This allows the mind to concentrate on sounds that might be more important.

Look, listen, and learn: Hearing is a vital part of the way children gain new information and understanding, especially at school and when talking with friends.

Try this!

Cup your hands over your ears, fingers together. Sounds are much quieter and more muffled because your hands block some sound waves. Then, rub your ears with your hands, and hear how loud these sounds are. The rubbing causes vibrations that pass directly through the skin and skull bone to the inner ear, without the need for sound waves.

Outer ear

The ear is much more than the part you can see on the side of the head. This outer section is the pinna, a flap of skin-covered cartilage. It funnels sound waves into the **ear canal,** a tube leading

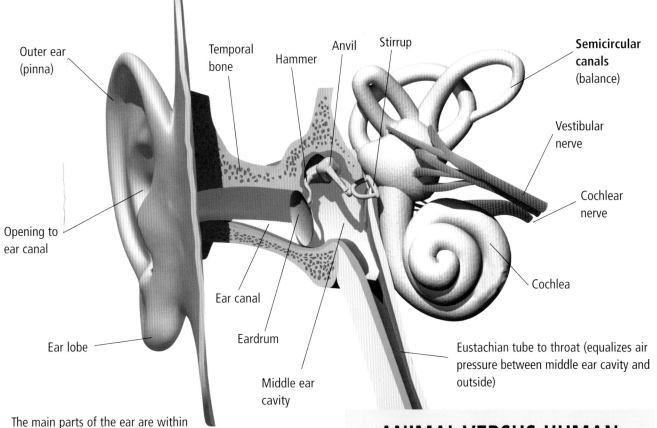

Outer ear
(pinna)

Temporal
bone

Hammer

Anvil

Stirrup

**Semicircular
canals**
(balance)

Vestibular
nerve

Cochlear
nerve

Opening to
ear canal

Ear canal

Cochlea

Ear lobe

Eardrum

Eustachian tube to throat (equalizes air
pressure between middle ear cavity and
outside)

Middle ear
cavity

The main parts of the ear are within
the thickness of the part of the skull
called the temporal bone.

about four-fifths of an inch (two
centimeters) into the skull bone. The
canal ends at the eardrum, a taut flap
of thin skin the size of the little
fingernail. Sound waves strike the
eardrum and make it shake.

Middle ear

On the inner side of the eardrum is the
middle ear cavity, containing three tiny
bones called the hammer, anvil, and
stirrup. These are the auditory **ossicles,**
the smallest bones in the body. They are
joined end-to-end, with the hammer
touching the eardrum and the stirrup
touching part of the inner ear called
the **cochlea.** Vibrations pass from the
eardrum along the ossicles to the
cochlea, where **nerve** signals are made.

ANIMAL VERSUS HUMAN

Human ears have limits. Some sounds are
too quiet, too high, or too deep for us to
hear. Certain animals, such as dogs and
horses, have better hearing than we do
and easily detect sounds that we cannot.

DEEP IN THE EAR

Changing patterns

Deep in the ear, patterns of sound vibrations are changed into patterns of **nerve** signals in the curled, snail-shaped part called the **cochlea.** This part is well protected by skull bone almost all around it. The stirrup bone vibrates against a thin, flexible part of the cochlea, the oval window. When the oval window vibrates, this sends ripples into the fluid inside the cochlea.

Semicircular canals
(balance)

Vestibular nerves (balance)

A small section cut out of the cochlea (left) is enlarged (below) to show the three passageways or ducts running through it, and the spiral organ of Corti, which is then enlarged further (opposite).

Cochlear nerve (hearing)

Basal whorl of cochlea

Duct system within cochlea

Utricle
(balance)

Apex (upper tip) of cochlea

Saccule
(balance)

ENLARGED VIEW OF COCHLEA

Upper duct   Organ of Corti

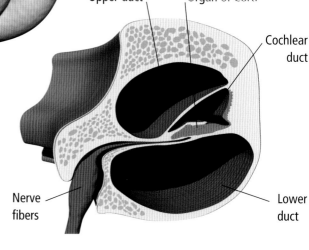

Cochlear duct

Nerve fibers

Lower duct

Top Tips

The **ear canal's** lining makes wax, which attracts dust and dirt. As the jaw joints near the ears move when speaking and chewing, the flakes of wax naturally work their way out of the canal. Very occasionally, too much wax or a tiny object gets stuck in the canal. A doctor or other medical worker should remove this. Never try to poke it out yourself, even with a cotton swab (Q-Tip), because you might damage the eardrum.

Micro-hairs

Inside the cochlea, curled around like a corkscrew, is the spiral organ of Corti. This has two main layers, or membranes, one on top of the other. The bottom one, the basilar membrane, has about 25,000 tiny cells called hair **cells** in

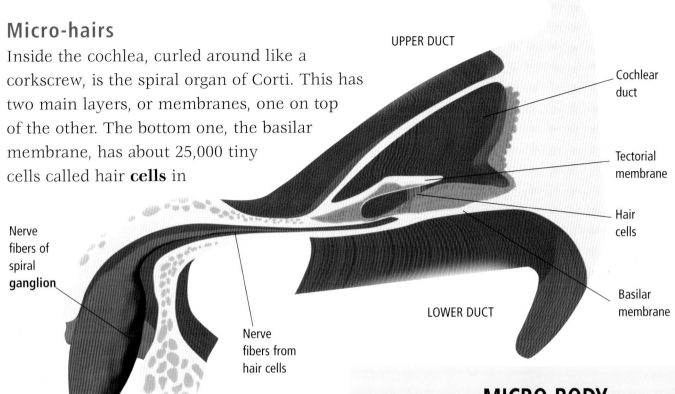

UPPER DUCT

Cochlear duct

Tectorial membrane

Hair cells

Basilar membrane

LOWER DUCT

Nerve fibers of spiral **ganglion**

Nerve fibers from hair cells

Inside the cochlea, the spiral organ of Corti has two membranes with thousands of hair cells between.

four rows along its length. Sticking up from each cell are 50 or more short micro-hairs. These hair tips project into the upper layer, the tectorial membrane.

Sounds to signals

Ripples from the sound vibrations pass through the fluid inside the cochlea. They cause the membranes to flex or bend up and down and the micro-hairs to shake. As the micro-hairs move, the hair cells from which they project make nerve signals. These pass along the hair cell nerve fibers, which gather together to become the cochlear nerve. The nerve carries the signals to the hearing center, or auditory **cortex,** on the side of the brain.

MICRO BODY

The hair cells in the organ of Corti are arranged in four rows. Three are outer hair cells and the micro-hairs of each one form a U-shaped pattern. The inner hair cells have their micro-hairs arranged in a line.

The micro-hairs of the hair cells stick into the tectorial membrane.

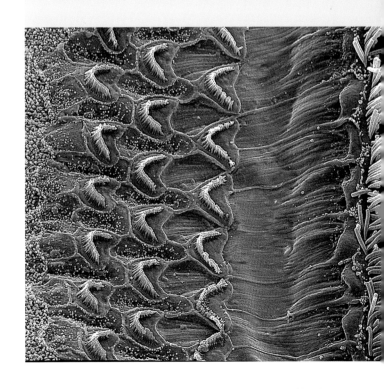

WHERE'S THAT NOISE?

In the rain forest, sight is very limited, but sounds can warn of approaching danger.

Sound identification

Imagine you are walking through a forest on a very dark night. You need to rely more on your ears than your eyes. Your mind concentrates on every tiny sound, figuring out its various features, trying to identify it and what it means. One feature is loudness or volume. Deep in the ear, in the **cochlea,** sound vibrations make the membranes and micro-hairs move. Louder sounds make bigger vibrations, and so the membranes and micro-hairs move farther, making more **nerve** signals.

Try this!

Many sounds reach the ear after bouncing, or reflecting, off surfaces such as walls and floors. In a room with hard walls and a hard floor (not carpeted), ask a friend to clap hands in different places—near the wall, high up, and low down. Stand in the middle of the room with your eyes closed. Hear how the claps differ in volume and how the sounds bounce or echo. Can you point to the correct direction of the clap each time?

High and low

Another feature of sound is pitch: the high or low quality of sound. Higher-pitched sounds make faster vibrations. Some parts of the cochlear membranes bend more with high-pitched sounds, while other parts are affected by low-pitched sounds. Like volume, pitch changes the patterns of nerve signals being sent to the brain.

Direction of sound

Sounds travel through air at about 360 yards (330 meters) per second. This means a sound coming from one side reaches the nearer ear a split second before it gets to the farther ear. Also, because it passes straight into the **ear canal** of the nearer ear, it is louder there, compared to the other ear canal facing the other direction. The brain detects these tiny differences in timing and loudness and figures out where a sound is coming from.

ANIMAL VERSUS HUMAN

Whales and dolphins use clicks, squeals, and groans to communicate messages. Water carries sound waves much faster and farther than air, and some whale songs travel more than 60 miles (100 kilometers) through the ocean. Imagine shouting that far on land.

Louder sounds (bigger waves) reach nearer ear first

Quieter sounds (smaller waves) reach farther ear later

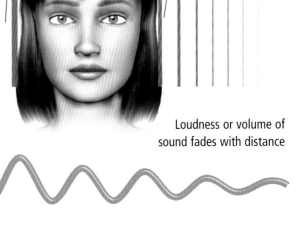

A sound that comes from one side is louder and earlier in the ear on that side compared to the other ear. The brain can detect the time difference, which is less than one-thousandth of a second.

Loudness or volume of sound fades with distance

HEARING PROBLEMS

Tests and treatment

Some people may not be aware that they have hearing difficulties. Signs of hearing loss include the need to turn up the television or stereo louder than other people and asking people to repeat what they have said when others have heard clearly. Simple tests by a doctor or other medical staff can check if there is a problem. Then, a specialist, known as an audiologist, can do further tests and suggest treatment, such as a hearing aid or, in some cases, surgery.

Ear infections

Sometimes germs multiply in the outer, middle, or inner ear. The germs that cause a sore throat can spread along a channel called the Eustachian tube from the back of the throat to the

Headphones are part of the vital protective equipment for many noisy jobs, such as grinding metal and sawing wood.

Top Tips

Sounds that are too loud, especially if high-pitched and long-lasting, can damage the internal ear's delicate structures, sometimes permanently. There are usually regulations to limit loud sounds in places such as nightclubs and factories. People who work with noisy machines and musicians often wear ear plugs or headphones to protect their hearing.

middle ear. There they cause a condition called otitis media, infecting the middle ear and making it swollen and filled with pus. This may press on and burst the eardrum. Germs that cause a common cold or sinus infection can also spread to the ear.

Glue ear

A long-term ear infection can leave sticky fluid in the middle ear. This "glue ear" may not cause much pain, but it can affect hearing by hampering the vibration of the ear bones. This can cause special problems during childhood, when children are learning to speak and to listen. Sometimes a child thought to have learning difficulties actually has glue ear or another hearing problem. Most ear infections clear up on their own, perhaps with the help of painkillers to treat the symptom of the earache. But severe infection may need antibiotic treatment or even surgery.

Hearing difficulty

In otosclerosis, bony growths restrict the movements of the stirrup, so that it cannot pass its vibrations to the **cochlea.** In this and certain other ear disorders, a hearing aid may help. The stirrup also can be freed by an operation, or even replaced with an artificial version. In the rare event of

severe cochlear damage, a cochlear implant can partly restore hearing, as long as there are still some intact **nerve** fibers. The implant is a tiny electronic device inserted into the inner ear and connected by wires to a receiver under the scalp. It detects vibrations and mainly helps the person to hear his or her own voice.

MICRO BODY

In one form of cochlear implant, a behind-the-ear microphone sends signals to a transmitter on the scalp, which passes them to a receiver within the head.

In this hearing aid, the implant is under the wheel-like transmitter.

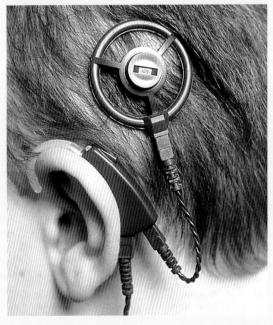

SMELL AND TASTE

Sniff the air

We usually notice the sense of smell (olfaction) less than other senses—that is, until we sniff a strong odor such as a powerful perfume or spoiled food. The nose detects common and everyday smells, but the brain often filters them out so that the mind can concentrate on new or changing odors that might be important.

For example, when you enter a place with a strong smell, like a flower store, your nose detects it. But then the smell seems to fade and may seem to disappear after a few minutes. The smell is still there and just as strong, but you have gotten used to it. This is known as habituation. It happens with sounds, touches, and also tastes.

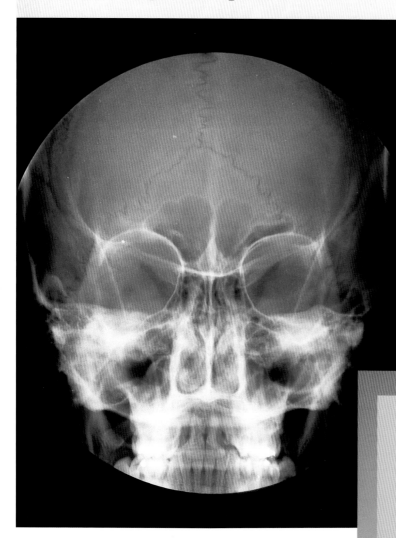

In this head X-ray, the nasal chambers show up as the dark regions between the lower parts of the eyes.

Try this!

When you breathe normally, air passes through the lower parts of the nasal chambers. Few odorant particles reach the olfactory areas in the upper part, so smells are weaker. If you sniff, air swirls higher into the roof of the nasal chamber, nearer the olfactory areas, so the smell is stronger. Try breathing normally near something with a very strong smell such as a flower, perfume, or air freshener, then sniff more deeply and see how much stronger the odor becomes.

Floating in air

Tiny **odorant** particles that are too small to see float about in the air. Every breath takes air into the nasal chambers, which are two thumb-sized air spaces in the skull, one behind each side of the nose. The parts that detect the odorant particles are in the lining of the top, or roof, of the nasal chamber. They are called the **olfactory** areas, or olfactory **epithelia** (see next page).

(see next page).

ANIMAL VERSUS HUMAN

Some animals rely more on their noses than on their eyes. The mole lives in darkness and its eyes are so tiny they are almost useless, but its nose is long and always sniffing for food or danger.

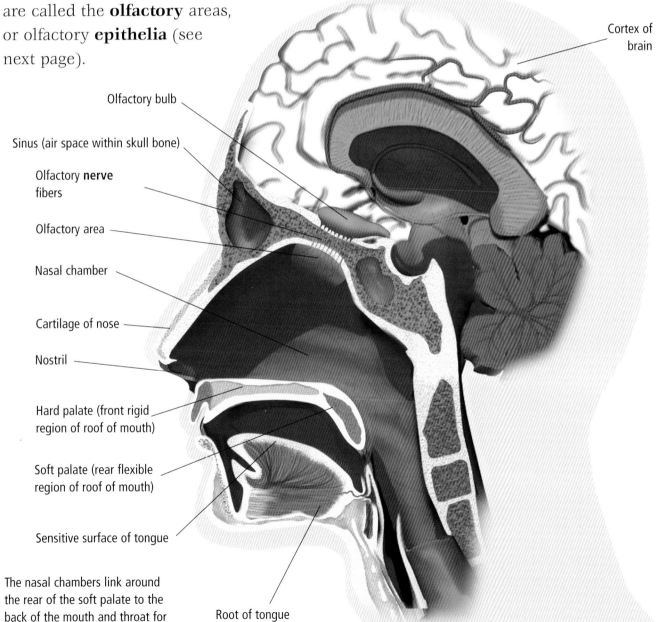

Cortex of brain

Olfactory bulb

Sinus (air space within skull bone)

Olfactory **nerve** fibers

Olfactory area

Nasal chamber

Cartilage of nose

Nostril

Hard palate (front rigid region of roof of mouth)

Soft palate (rear flexible region of roof of mouth)

Sensitive surface of tongue

The nasal chambers link around the rear of the soft palate to the back of the mouth and throat for breathing air.

Root of tongue

SCENTS, SENSE, AND GOOD TASTE

Olfactory cells

Each **olfactory** area is about the size of a thumbnail, containing about 20 million microscopic **cells** called olfactory cells. Each cell has 10 to 20 micro-hairs, called **cilia,** sticking out from its surface. The cilia project into the thin layer of **mucus** (slimy fluid) that coats the whole inner lining of the nasal chamber.

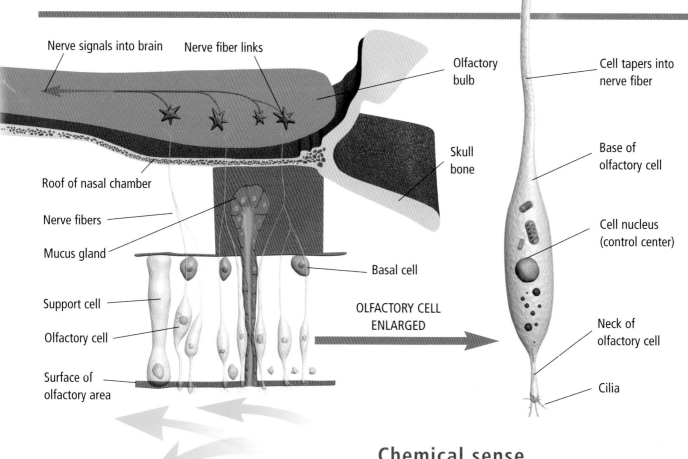

Nerve signals into brain

Nerve fiber links

Olfactory bulb

Cell tapers into nerve fiber

Roof of nasal chamber

Skull bone

Base of olfactory cell

Nerve fibers

Mucus gland

Cell nucleus (control center)

Basal cell

Support cell

OLFACTORY CELL ENLARGED

Olfactory cell

Neck of olfactory cell

Surface of olfactory area

Cilia

Odor particles in nasal chamber

The olfactory area contains thousands of olfactory cells, support cells, and other kinds of cells. The microscopic hairlike cilia of each olfactory cell hang from its surface into the air stream within the nasal chamber below.

Chemical sense

Smell is a chemosense, which means it is a body sense that detects chemicals, or the tiny floating particles called **odorants.** Each type of smell is probably carried by a different type of odorant chemical with its own shape. These

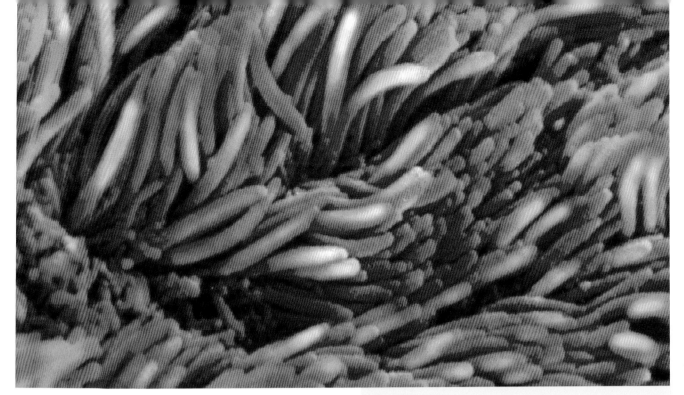

The mucus coating the smell-detecting cilia has been removed in this microphotograph.

particles fit into receptors, or "landing sites," that cover the cilia that hang down from the olfactory cells. If a particular odorant chemical fits into a same-shaped receptor, like a key into a lock, this causes the olfactory cell to make nerve signals.

To the brain

Like other sense organs, the olfactory areas send signals along nerve fibers. These pass through the thin layer of skull bone just above to a large, bulging collection of nerves under the front of the brain that is known as the olfactory bulb. Here the signals are partly sorted and combined before traveling along the olfactory nerve into the brain itself.

MICRO BODY

The microscopic cilia that project from the twenty-plus million olfactory cells form a thick "carpet" that is coated with slimy mucus. Odorant particles must seep or dissolve into the mucus before they can fit into "landing sites," or receptors, on the cilia, and thereby generate **nerve** signals.

Try this!

Have you ever smelled something and had a strong memory about it? Smells often provoke strong memories. This may be because the memory and smell centers in the brain are near each other and have many connections between them.

TIP OF THE TONGUE

Safety checks

Taste (gustation) is, like smell, a chemosense. The tongue detects tiny particles of chemicals called flavorants in foods and drinks. Like smell, taste allows us to check foods before we eat them. If a food smells and tastes odd or unusual, we tend to avoid it. Long ago when foods were gathered from the wild, this was a useful way of checking whether berries, fruits, and other items were safe to eat. Today smell and taste are used more for pleasure, as we enjoy our meals, snacks, and drinks.

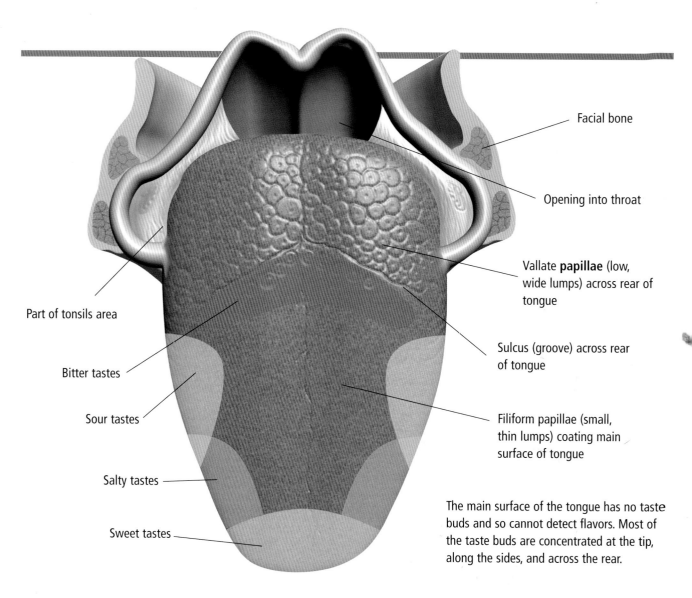

Facial bone

Opening into throat

Vallate **papillae** (low, wide lumps) across rear of tongue

Sulcus (groove) across rear of tongue

Part of tonsils area

Bitter tastes

Sour tastes

Filiform papillae (small, thin lumps) coating main surface of tongue

Salty tastes

Sweet tastes

The main surface of the tongue has no taste buds and so cannot detect flavors. Most of the taste buds are concentrated at the tip, along the sides, and across the rear.

Fewer flavors than odors

Tastes are detected by microscopic taste buds (see next page) spread along the sides and back of the tongue. They work in a similar way to the **olfactory cells** in the nose. However, they tell apart only four basic flavors: sweet, salty, sour, and bitter. All other flavors are combinations of these four, in varying amounts. In contrast, the nose can tell apart many thousands of different smells. The nose also helps with taste.

Try this!

You will need a drinking straw, some sugar, and clean water to rinse your mouth between each test. Use the straw to put a few grains of sugar on the tip of your tongue, but do not move your tongue. Can you detect the sweet flavor? After rinsing, put some grains on the side of your tongue. Is the sweetness as strong? Try the back of your tongue. Can you detect any sweetness at all? The diagram opposite shows which part of the tongue is sensitive to sugar.

ANIMAL VERSUS HUMAN

Since an anteater can hardly open or close its small jaws, it eats with its tongue. It licks up insects that stick to the mucus coating its very long tongue. It's tongue can be up to 24 inches (60 centimeters).

TASTE BUDS

Gripping and tasting

The tongue has small pimple-like lumps called **papillae** over much of its surface. These papillae help the tongue to grip slippery food as it is mixed with **saliva** (spit) and chewed. The taste buds, the parts of the tongue that do the tasting are much smaller than the papillae. There are about 10,000 microscopic taste buds. Most of the taste buds are around the sides and bases of the papillae, along the edges of the tongue, and across its rear. There are also a few taste buds on the insides of the cheeks and lips. The main central area of the tongue has no taste buds, and so it cannot detect any flavors.

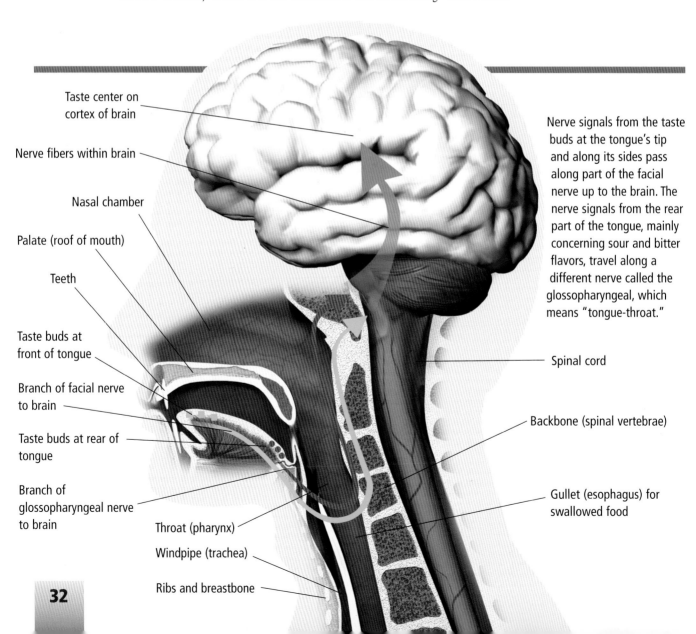

Taste center on cortex of brain

Nerve fibers within brain

Nasal chamber

Palate (roof of mouth)

Teeth

Taste buds at front of tongue

Branch of facial nerve to brain

Taste buds at rear of tongue

Branch of glossopharyngeal nerve to brain

Throat (pharynx)

Windpipe (trachea)

Ribs and breastbone

Nerve signals from the taste buds at the tongue's tip and along its sides pass along part of the facial nerve up to the brain. The nerve signals from the rear part of the tongue, mainly concerning sour and bitter flavors, travel along a different nerve called the glossopharyngeal, which means "tongue-throat."

Spinal cord

Backbone (spinal vertebrae)

Gullet (esophagus) for swallowed food

Another chemosense

Each taste bud is like a tiny orange, with about 50 **cells** as the segments. Half of these are **gustatory,** or taste-sensing cells, and each one has several micro-hairs, **cilia,** sticking out from its tip. Particular shapes of flavorant particles in food fit into the same-shaped receptors, or "landing sites," on the cilia, like keys into their locks, and this makes the gustatory cell produce **nerve** signals. The signals pass along nerve fibers to the taste areas on each side of the brain, called the gustatory **cortex.**

Flavor particles dissolved in saliva seep through tiny holes in the tongue's surface, called taste pores, to reach the taste buds below. The hairlike cilia at the upper end of each gustatory cell detect the particles.

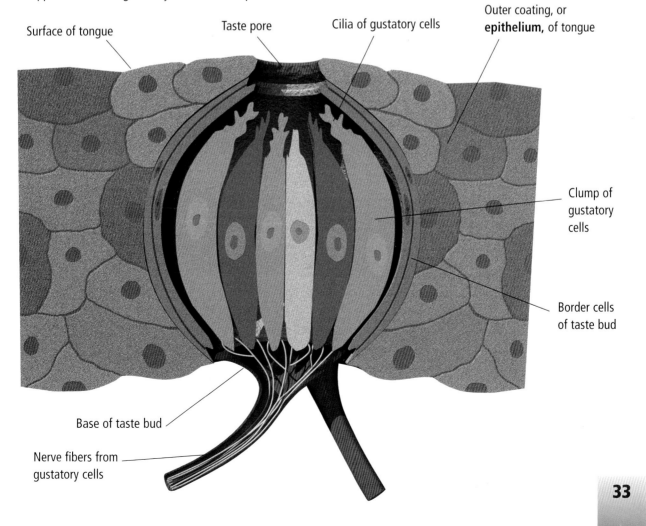

Surface of tongue

Taste pore

Cilia of gustatory cells

Outer coating, or **epithelium,** of tongue

Clump of gustatory cells

Border cells of taste bud

Base of taste bud

Nerve fibers from gustatory cells

SMELL AND TASTE PROBLEMS

Strongly linked

Smell and taste are separate senses, and their **nerve** signals travel to different parts of the brain. But these senses work together when we eat and drink. Also, odors from chewed food float up from the back of the mouth, around the rear of the palate, and into the nasal chamber, where they are smelled. For this reason, odors and flavors become strongly linked in the mind. What we imagine as the "taste" of a food is a combination of taste and smell. When a common cold blocks the nose, it cannot detect food odors. Then, it seems like food has little taste. In fact it tastes normal, but the added interest of its smells is missing.

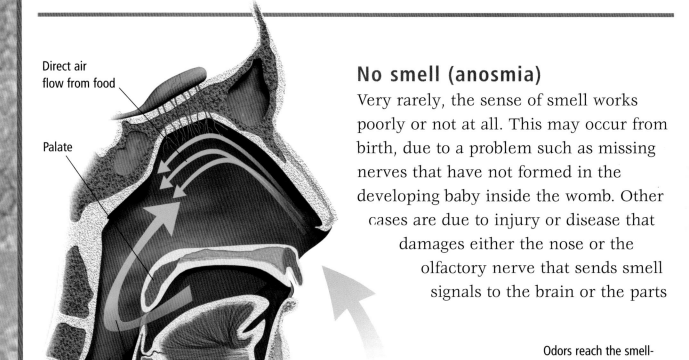

Direct air flow from food

Palate

Throat

Indirect air flow from food being chewed in the mouth

Inhaled **odorants**

No smell (anosmia)

Very rarely, the sense of smell works poorly or not at all. This may occur from birth, due to a problem such as missing nerves that have not formed in the developing baby inside the womb. Other cases are due to injury or disease that damages either the nose or the olfactory nerve that sends smell signals to the brain or the parts

Odors reach the smell-detecting area inside the nose both from breathed-in air and from air floating up around the back of the palate.

of the brain where smell signals are analyzed. The same can happen with taste.

Sensing nothing

Some medicines and also some mental (mind-based) conditions can affect the way the brain deals with smells, tastes, or other senses. The sense may seem blunted and duller, or sharper and "heightened." The mind can be tricked into experiencing odors, flavors, sights, sounds, or touches that do not exist. These are called sensory hallucinations.

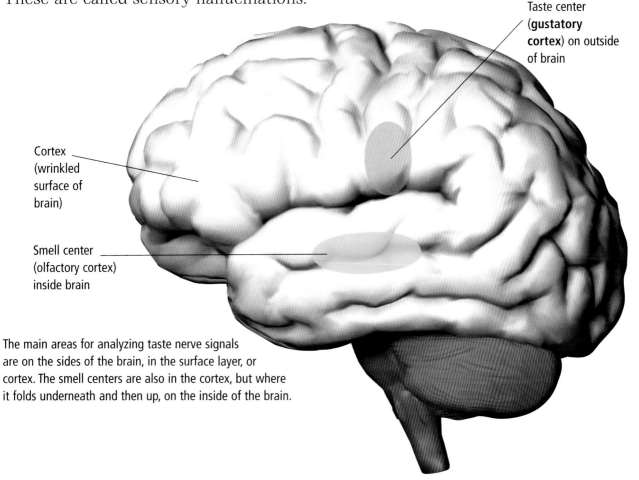

Taste center (**gustatory cortex**) on outside of brain

Cortex (wrinkled surface of brain)

Smell center (olfactory cortex) inside brain

The main areas for analyzing taste nerve signals are on the sides of the brain, in the surface layer, or cortex. The smell centers are also in the cortex, but where it folds underneath and then up, on the inside of the brain.

THE SENSE OF TOUCH

Strange feelings

Touch one of your hands with the fingertips of the other. The hand feels warm, dry, and slightly soft. Dip the hand in cold water and try again. Now it feels cooler, wet, and slippery. The sense of touch provides far more information than whether part of the body is in contact with something. It distinguishes hard from soft, rough from smooth, warm from cold, wet from dry, sticky from slippery, and still from moving.

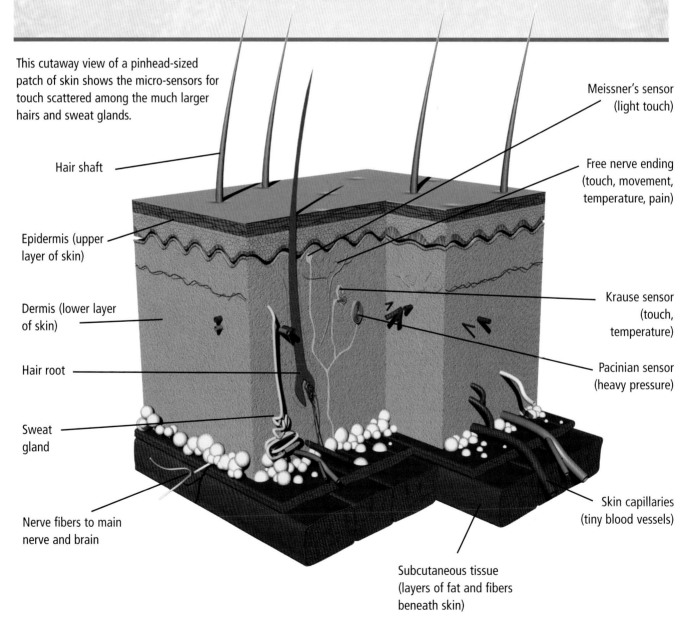

This cutaway view of a pinhead-sized patch of skin shows the micro-sensors for touch scattered among the much larger hairs and sweat glands.

Hair shaft

Epidermis (upper layer of skin)

Dermis (lower layer of skin)

Hair root

Sweat gland

Nerve fibers to main nerve and brain

Meissner's sensor (light touch)

Free nerve ending (touch, movement, temperature, pain)

Krause sensor (touch, temperature)

Pacinian sensor (heavy pressure)

Skin capillaries (tiny blood vessels)

Subcutaneous tissue (layers of fat and fibers beneath skin)

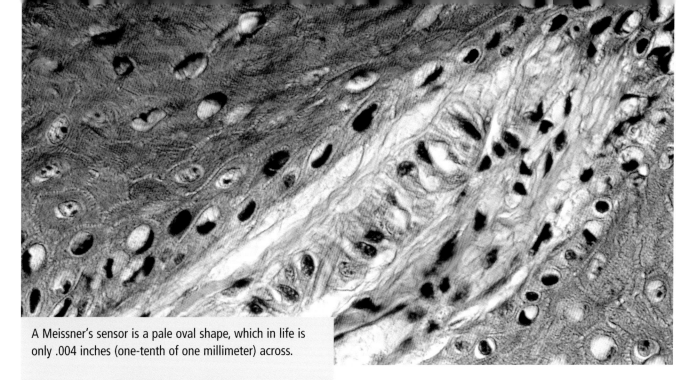

A Meissner's sensor is a pale oval shape, which in life is only .004 inches (one-tenth of one millimeter) across.

MICRO BODY

The different microsensors in skin are placed at different levels, according to the type of touch they detect. Meissner's sensors are near the surface and respond to very light pressure. Pacinian sensors detect heavier pressure and are lower down.

Microsensors

Skin protects the body from knocks, harmful rays, and germs, keeps in body fluids, and stops the body from getting too hot or cold. But skin is also the main touch organ of the body. An area of skin the size of a fingernail has up to one million microscopic touch sensors. These are the specially shaped ends of **nerve** fibers, situated just under the surface. There are at least seven main kinds of sensors. The largest are the size of a pinhead, but most are thousands of times smaller. Each detects different features of touch. Some respond to very light contact, others to heavier pressure or heat, cold, or vibrations. Still other kinds of sensors respond to all of these. The sensors send complicated patterns of nerve signals to the brain. A strip-shaped area on either side of the brain's surface, the touch center, or **somato-sensory cortex,** figures out the type of object or substance that is being touched.

Try this!

Very carefully, move a tiny hair on your arm without contacting the skin there. Can you feel anything? The hair itself is dead and has no sense of touch. But wrapped around its base, in the skin, are sensitive nerve endings. They detect that hair's movement. When a strong wind blows on the skin, we feel it because it moves the tiny hairs there.

WHAT A PAIN!

A vital warning

Pain is perhaps the most unwelcome of the body's sensations, yet it is vital. It warns that a body part is damaged or injured. Pain tells us to be careful and to limit the damage so that the part can heal itself. If we ignore the pain of a wound in the skin, the wound may worsen and, left open, become infected with germs. If we take no note of the pain in a damaged joint, we may continue to use the joint rather than rest it, increasing the harm.

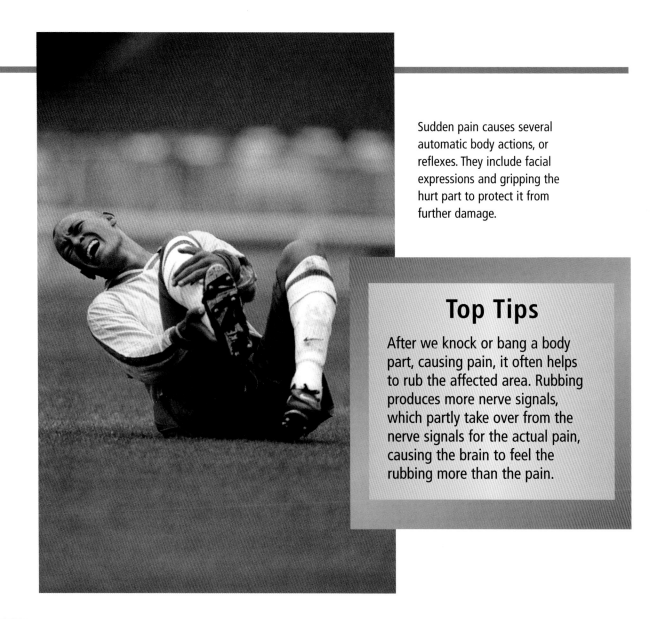

Sudden pain causes several automatic body actions, or reflexes. They include facial expressions and gripping the hurt part to protect it from further damage.

Top Tips

After we knock or bang a body part, causing pain, it often helps to rub the affected area. Rubbing produces more nerve signals, which partly take over from the nerve signals for the actual pain, causing the brain to feel the rubbing more than the pain.

Pain all over

Pain is part of the sense of touch, based in the skin. It can also occur in almost any body part: in joints, muscles, blood vessels, the stomach, **nerves,** even deep inside bones. All of these parts have microscopic nerve fiber endings specialized to detect damage around them. These are shaped like tiny branching trees and called free nerve endings. Oddly, the only part of the body that lacks these pain sensors is the brain, and so the brain detects pain in other body parts but cannot feel any damage or harm to itself.

Types of pain

No one can experience the pain felt by another person. But we can describe our pain to others with words such as sharp, shooting, burning, crushing, cramping, dull, aching, and throbbing. We can also say if a pain comes and goes or is there all the time, and whether it stops us from doing anything. It is important to describe all of these aspects of pain clearly to a doctor or other medical professional, since the description can give clues to the cause and extent of the underlying problem.

MICRO BODY

Free nerve endings are the tiny, branching ends of nerve fibers. They are found in most body parts and detect not only pain but also heat, cold, and movements.

The treelike branches of a free nerve ending pass through the skin, waiting to respond to any damage.

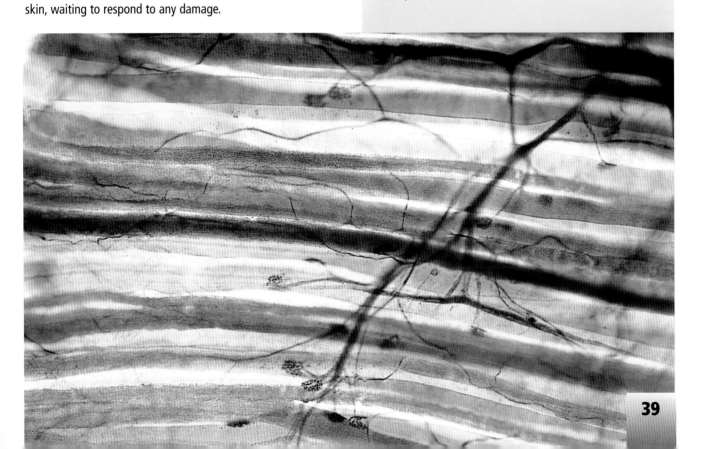

BALANCE

A continuous process

Balance is sometimes called the "sixth sense." But it is really a body process that goes on all the time, using information from various sense organs.

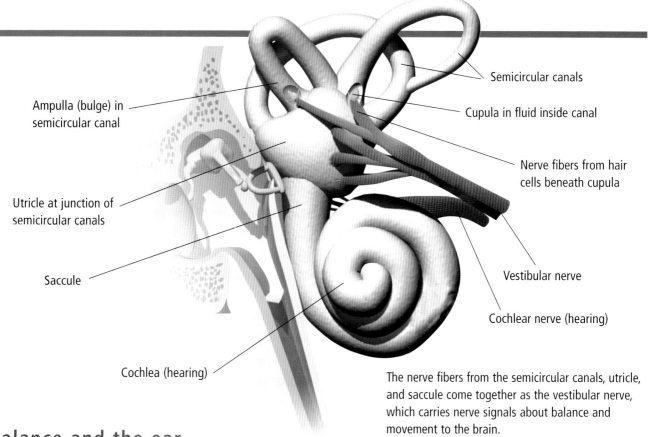

Semicircular canals

Cupula in fluid inside canal

Nerve fibers from hair cells beneath cupula

Ampulla (bulge) in semicircular canal

Utricle at junction of semicircular canals

Saccule

Vestibular nerve

Cochlear nerve (hearing)

Cochlea (hearing)

The nerve fibers from the semicircular canals, utricle, and saccule come together as the vestibular nerve, which carries nerve signals about balance and movement to the brain.

Balance and the ear

Inside the ear and joined to the **cochlea** are bulging parts, called the **utricle** and **saccule,** and three C-shaped tubes, called the **semicircular canals.** Like the cochlea, these are filled with fluid. The utricle and saccule contain jellylike lumps of tiny, heavy crystals called otoconia. Microscopic hair **cells,** like those in the cochlea, have tiny hairs that stick into these lumps. The force of gravity pulls the lumps down. As the head changes position, the angle of pull alters, moving the micro-hairs so that their cells send **nerve** signals to the brain.

Each semicircular canal also has a bulge near one end, containing another patch of hair cells. Their micro-hairs stick into another jellylike lump, the cupula. As the head twists and turns, the fluid in each

canal swishes back and forth. This pushes the cupula, which pulls on the hair cells and so makes nerve signals. The three canals are at right angles to each other, so any head movement—up-and-down, side-to-side, front-and-back—affects one or more of the canals.

Other aspects of balance

Sight and touch help balance. The eyes see horizontal surfaces such as floors and water surfaces, and vertical ones such as walls and tree trunks. As the head tilts, these change angles, and the brain notes this. Also, as the body leans, pressure on the feet and other body parts alters, and again the brain receives information about this (see next page). From all these sensory inputs, the brain figures out the position and movement of the body and instructs muscles to keep it poised and "well-balanced."

Try this!

Stand up straight and close your eyes. Gradually you may feel your body start to lean or sway. Your brain has lost the set of sensory inputs from your eyes that help with balance. Staying upright becomes slightly more difficult, and soon you want to open your eyes again.

Problems with balance

When you cannot control your balance, for instance on an amusement park ride, the messages going to your brain can make you feel dizzy and sick. Inner ear infections can also affect the balance organs and can cause the same sorts of symptoms.

Jet pilots train to become used to sudden changes in direction and position so that their balance will be less affected.

A sense of position

Do you know, without looking at your hand, what position it is in? Is your wrist straight, and are your fingers together or spread apart? Somehow you "know" the position of a body part, even though you cannot see it. This positional sense is called **proprioception,** or the kinesthetic sense. It tells the brain about the position or posture of each part. This sense comes from millions of microscopic sensors throughout the body that are linked to the brain by **nerves.**

The brain can detect the positions and tiny movements of the fingers without seeing, using the proprioceptive sense. An example of this is musician Stevie Wonder, who has no vision.

Top Tips

When a body part has stayed in the same position for a long time, it is good to stretch and bend it. This prevents blood vessels and nerves from becoming kinked, relieves tension in muscles and joints, and helps the proprioceptive sensors to "update" the brain about the body's posture.

Sprays and spindles

Proprioceptive sensors are less than .004 inches (one-tenth of one millimeter) in size, and they have various names and shapes. They include "spray" nerve endings shaped like little trees, "corpuscle" nerve endings that are round with layers (like tiny onions), and "spindle" nerve endings that are long and tapering. These sensors are especially common in muscles and joints. They constantly detect the amount of pull or stretch, which alters as the body moves, and send their nerve signals to the brain.

Squash and stretch

The information from this inner proprioceptive sense is especially important in providing information for balance. For example, as you stand up and lean forward, the pressure on the front of your feet increases, and you feel this in the skin on the foot. But the sensors in the muscles and joints also respond by feeling the pressure all the way up the front of your feet, legs, and torso. Meanwhile, the muscles around the back of the legs and torso are slightly stretched. Proprioceptive sensors detect all this and inform the brain.

Outer layer (gray matter, or **cortex**)

Inner layer (white matter of nerve fibers)

Nerve fiber connections in cerebellum

Movement center, or motor cortex, on brain's surface

Nerve fibers within brain

Cerebellum (movement coordination)

This cutaway view inside the brain, seen from the front of the body, shows how nerve fibers connect various parts such as the cortex and cerebellum, conveying nerve signals about proprioception.

Signals up and down spinal cord

A FIVE-SENSES EXPERIENCE

Mmmm ... delicious!

Next time you start eating a tasty meal, pause for a moment. Your enjoyment of food comes from your senses, and they all work alongside each other during the eating experience. The first hint of food might be the odors of cooking, which float from the oven through the air to your nose, even if you are some distance away. As explained earlier, smells can cause powerful reactions. The odor of food often makes the body prepare to eat by causing the release of **saliva** into the mouth, making it ready for chewing. This is why we say a meal "smells mouthwatering." You can also hear the sounds of cooking, such as the crackle and spit of the grill. Sounds and smells are useful because they carry from room to room, from places that the eyes cannot see.

More and more senses

Experienced cooks often say that we "eat with our eyes." If a meal looks well presented and appetizing, we are more likely to enjoy it. Sight is also very important for checking the meal. For example, if the peas on a

Are you feeling hungry? Even the sight of food in a photograph can tempt the appetite and make us ready to eat.

plate were blue or the baked beans were green, we would be suspicious. Then, as we start to eat, the food is chewed and mixed with saliva, which releases more **odorant** and **flavorant** substances, so tastes and smells combine for further enjoyment.

Touch is involved, too. There are microsensors, similar to those in the skin, on the lips, tongue, and gums, and in the lining of the cheeks and other mouth parts. These enable us to feel whether the food is hot or cold, hard or squishy, and other features of its texture or consistency. A meal is a full five-senses experience. It shows how the body's senses are vital for our pleasure and enjoyment, but also vital to our basic survival, since the senses help us to discover information and know what is happening around us.

ANIMAL VERSUS HUMAN

The human body has deep-seated reactions and instincts to avoid certain foods, especially old, rotting meat. But wild creatures such as the leopard are adapted to cope with such meals. This big cat may leave part of its prey, such as a gazelle, in a tree for a week or two in the hot sun and then come back to eat the decaying, smelly meat.

GLOSSARY

cell single unit, or "building block," of life, the human body is made of billions of cells of many different kinds

cilia microscopic, hairlike parts that can waft or wave back and forth, such as those lining the nasal chambers inside the nose

cochlea small, snail-shaped part deep inside the ear that changes the vibrations of sounds into nerve signals

cone short, tapering cell in the retina of the eye, specialized to make nerve signals when various colors of light fall on it

convergence in eyesight, when the eyes turn or swivel inward slightly so they both look directly at a nearby object

cornea transparent outer layer of the eyeball covering the iris and pupil and allowing light into the eye

cortex outermost wrinkled layer of the brain, where most conscious thoughts and sensations happen

ear canal tube or tunnel leading from the outer ear on the side of the head inward to the eardrum

epithelium (more than one are epithelia) layer covering the surface of a body part or forming its inner lining

fovea small area in the middle of the retina where the most cone cells are packed; and where vision is the most sharp and clear

ganglion lumplike part of a nerve that contains a group or gathering of the cell bodies from nerve cells

gustatory having to do with the sense of taste

humor general name for a liquid or fluid in the body, such as vitreous humor (the clear, jellylike fluid inside the eyeball)

iris colored ring-shaped muscle at the front of the eye, with a hole in the middle called the pupil

mucus general name for various thick, slimy, gooey fluids made by the body, produced especially to coat and protect the surfaces of its inner parts

nerve long, thin, stringlike parts inside the body that carry information in the form of nerve impulses or signals

odorants tiny particles of substances or chemicals, too small to see, that float in the air and stimulate the olfactory cells in the nose to give us the sensation of smell

olfactory having to do with the sense of smell

optic having to do with the sense of sight

optometrist doctor who focuses on diagnosing vision problems and prescribing glasses. An ophthamologist is a doctor who specializes in eyes and diseases of the eye. An optician is someone who makes glasses or contact lenses. The three are often confused.

ossicles three tiny bones deep in each ear that pass vibrations from the eardrum to the cochlea

papillae small lump- or pimple-like parts on the surface of a body part such as the tongue

proprioception sensory process within the body that tells us the position, angle, and posture of body parts such as the fingers, hands, arms, back, and legs

pupil hole in the iris at the front of the eye that lets light into the eyeball

retina very thin, bowl-shaped layer inside the rear of the eyeball that detects patterns of light rays and makes nerve signals

rod long, thin cell in the retina of the eye, specialized to make nerve signals when light falls on it

saccule bag-shaped part filled with fluid deep in the ear that senses the movements of the head and makes nerve signals

saliva watery liquid made by six salivary glands, it moistens the mouth and pours onto food to help chewing and swallowing

sclera tough outer covering of the eyeball

semicircular canals three C-shaped tubes filled with fluid deep in the ear that sense the movements of the head and make nerve signals

somato-sensory cortex parts on the cortex (outer surface) of the brain that receive and analyze nerve signals about touch and feeling from the skin

utricle box-shaped part filled with fluid deep in the ear that senses the movements of the head and makes nerve signals

FURTHER INFORMATION

BOOKS

Baldwin, Carol. *Health Matters: Hearing Loss.* Chicago: Heinemann, 2002.

Ballard, Carol. *Ears.* Chicago: Heinemann, 2003.

Ballard, Carol. *Eyes.* Chicago, Heinemann, 2003.

Silverstein, Alvin. *Smelling and Tasting.* New York: Millbrook, 2002.

Silverstein, Alvin. *Touching and Feeling.* New York: Millbrook, 2002.

Simon, Seymour. *Eyes and Ears.* New York: Morrow, 2003.

ORGANIZATIONS

American Association of People with Disabilities
1629 K Street, NW
Suite 503
Washington, DC 20006
(800) 840-8844
www.aapd.com

American Council of the Blind
1155 115th Street, NW
Suite 720
Washington, DC 20005
(800) 424-8666
www.acb.org

American Society for Deaf Children
P.O. Box 3355
Gettysburg, PA 17325
(717) 334-7922
www.deafchildren.org

INDEX